Country's Newest Stars

CHRIS STAPLETON

Tammy Gagne

Mitchell Lane
PUBLISHERS
2001 SW 31st Avenue
Hallandale, FL 33009
www.mitchelllane.com

Mitchell Lane
PUBLISHERS

Printing   1   2   3   4   5   6   7   8   9

Brett Eldridge
Chris Stapleton
Dierks Bentley

Eric Church
Jake Owen
Kacey Musgraves

Designer: Sharon Beck
Editor: Jim Whiting

Library of Congress Cataloging-in-Publication Data
Names: Gagne, Tammy, author.
Title: Chris Stapleton / by Tammy Gagne.
Description: Hallandale, FL : Mitchell Lane Publishers, [2018] | Series: Country's newest stars | Includes bibliographical references and index.
Identifiers: LCCN 2017046714 | ISBN 9781680201543 (library bound)
Subjects: LCSH: Stapleton, Chris, 1978– —Juvenile literature. | Country musicians—United States—Biography—Juvenile literature.
Classification: LCC ML3930.S73 G34 2018 | DDC 782.421642092 [B] —dc23
LC record available at https://lccn.loc.gov/2017046714

eBook ISBN: 9-781-68020-155-0

ABOUT THE AUTHOR: Tammy Gagne has written more than 200 books for both adults and children. Her recent titles include several books about country music artists—including *Eric Church* and *Kacey Musgraves*. She resides in northern New England with her husband and son.

PHOTO CREDITS: Design elements: (vintage paper guitar lake scene)—RhaStudio/iStock/Getty Images Plus, (star)—Andre_/DigitalVision Vectors/Getty Images, (abstract grunge)—Chen Ping-hung/Hemera/Getty Images Plus, (Contents background)—bobvidler/DigitalVision Vectors, (back matter banner)— fatmayilmaz/DigitalVision Vectors; cover, pp. 1, 25—Kevin Winter/Staff/Getty Images Entertainment; p. 4—Jason Moore/ZUMA Wire/Alamy Live News/ZUMA Press, Inc./Alamy Stock Photo; p. 6—OnInnovation/cc-by-nd 2.0; p. 7—Julio Enriquez/cc-by-sa 2.0; p. 8—Jason Davis/Stringer/Getty Images Entertainment; pp. 9, 11—Rick Diamond/Staff/Getty Images Entertainment; p. 12— Corkythehornetfan/cc-by-sa 4.0; p. 13—Boston Public Library Tichnor Brothers collection/Public domain; p. 15—Kevork Djansezian/Stringer/Getty Images Entertainment; p. 16—Michael Loccisano/Staff/Getty Images Entertainment; p. 20—Dia Dipasupil/Staff/Getty Images Entertainment; p. 21—Ethan Miller/Staff/Getty Images Entertainment; pp. 22-23—John Shearer/Country Rising/Handout/Getty Images Entertainment; p. 27—ABC/Image Group LA/cc-by-nd 2.0.

CONTENTS

A Hard-Working Musician

"**C**an anyone tell me the definition of an overnight success?" Ms. Rawson asked her first-period social studies class. Connor's hand sprang up before his teacher called on him. He loved Ms. Rawson's class. Even more, he loved it when he knew the answers to her questions. Social studies was his second-favorite subject. The only thing he liked better was music.

"Isn't it someone who becomes successful right away without having to work too hard or long?" he asked.

"Exactly," Ms. Rawson answered. "Now, can anyone name an overnight success? Just shout out the name of someone you think fits this description."

Connor could barely hear the names as his friends took their teacher literally, yelling them as loudly as they could. A few hollered the names of sports stars. Others

> Alicia loved social studies as much as Connor. She was also the only student who had a higher grade than he did.

Chris Stapleton performs at the American Roots Music and Arts Festival in 2015. The event took place at the Walnut Creek Ampitheatre in Raleigh, North Carolina.

named famous actors and reality television stars. When it seemed like they were all done, Alicia added someone a little different.

"Elon Musk," she said at a normal volume. Alicia loved social studies as much as Connor. She was also the only student who had a higher grade than he did. Ms. Rawson held a contest each year. The student with the

"**How about that singer who won all of those country music awards—Chris Stapleton?**"

highest grade in her class didn't have to take the final exam. Connor was sure that Alicia would be the winner.

"Hmmm," Ms. Rawson replied. "Interesting choices. Let's start with that last one.

"Why do you think Elon Musk was an overnight success, Alicia?"

"Because it seems like no one knew who he was when all of sudden he became one of the most famous engineers in the world for his work with electric cars."

"I can see why you would choose him," the teacher responded. "A few years ago most of us had no idea who Elon Musk was. But did you know that he spent more than a decade studying physics and battery technology before he started Tesla? Sometimes what seems like overnight success is a lot of hard work that people don't talk about as much. The truth is that there are very few genuine overnight successes."

Alicia tried again. "How about that singer who won all of those country music awards—Chris Stapleton? I heard that he came out of nowhere to beat out all of the other artists who had been around much longer."

Elon Musk

This time it was Connor who replied to Alicia. "Actually, Chris Stapleton has also been around for a lot longer than most people realize."

"Tell us more," Ms. Rawson instructed, excited to see her students engaged in the discussion she had started.

"I wrote a paper about Chris Stapleton for music class last year," Connor explained. "He has been making a living in country music since 2001. Musicians like Kenny Chesney, Thomas Rhett, and even Adele have recorded his songs. He has written more than 200 songs that other singers have recorded. Six of them have gone all the way to number one on the charts. One article I found said he has written more than a thousand songs in all."

"Interesting!" Ms. Rawson exclaimed. "It sounds like all his hard work paid off, just like Elon Musk's has." As his teacher went on to explain how success of all kinds takes great effort, Connor's mind wandered to his social studies grade. Perhaps he could end up with the highest grade in the class by the end of the year. He was certainly willing to put the hard work into it.

He has written more than 200 songs that other singers have recorded.

Rising Up the Charts—Twice

Chris Stapleton has definitely made a name for himself in the world of country music. In 2015, he released *Traveller*, his first country music album. Listeners obviously enjoyed hearing Chris perform his own songs as much as they liked hearing other artists singing them. The album did well. Critics praised both his songwriting and vocal talents.

November 4, 2015 was a big night for Chris Stapleton. He proudly holds his three CMA awards.

Chris was nominated for three awards at the 2015 Country Music Awards—New Artist of the Year, Album of the Year, and Male Vocalist of the Year. The nominations alone were mighty impressive for a musician who had just released his first solo album in May. What was even more remarkable was that Chris won all three of these awards! "This is an unbelievable thing, and I'm not going to take it lightly," he promised in his acceptance speech for the final honor of the evening.

His success also led to an invitation to perform at the awards ceremony. Chris appeared on stage with his friend and fellow musician Justin Timberlake. They played a cover of George Jones's "Tennessee Whiskey" and Timberlake's "Drink You Away." Although *Traveller* had already been out for six months, it re-entered the music charts following the duet. This time, though, the album did not just rise up the country music charts. It took the number one spot in all genres!

Chris was nominated for three awards at the 2015 Country Music Awards—New Artist of the Year, Album of the Year, and Male Vocalist of the Year.

Chris Stapleton's live performance with Justin Timberlake at the 2015 CMA Awards helped him skyrocket to the top of the music charts.

The Old Ways

Christopher Alvin Stapleton was born on April 15, 1978 in Lexington, Kentucky. Eight years earlier, Loretta Lynn topped the country music charts with her song "Coal Miner's Daughter." Chris could have written a song about his own life as a coal miner's son. His father Herbert was an electrical engineer in the coal mines of Kentucky. His mother Carol worked as a dietician before becoming a stay-at-home mom. Chris grew up in the small town of Staffordsville with an older brother, Herbert, and a younger sister, Melanie.

Chris credits his father with introducing him to country music. He used to listen to classic country singers such as Waylon Jennings and Willie Nelson while riding in the car with his dad. He remembers how his father loved turning the volume up high while driving. His dad also played a

Chris grew up in the small town of Staffordsville with an older brother, Herbert, and a younger sister, Melanie.

Chris and his wife, Morgane Stapleton, are both musicians. They are pictured here at the 50th Annual ASCAP Country Music Awards in 2012.

lot of classic R&B music by legends such as Ray Charles and Aretha Franklin.

These artists influenced Chris as he became a songwriter as an adult. People often say he has an "old country" style. He doesn't mind this description at all. He openly admits that he likes the old ways of doing things. When asked why he spelled *Traveller* with two "l"s on his first album, Chris explained that when a word has two spellings, he prefers the older one.

CHAPTER 2

When it came time to record that first album, Chris wanted to honor the traditional style of country that he listened to while growing up. One of the ways he accomplished this was by using some of the same musicians who had played with his idols. Guitarist Robby Turner had played with Waylon Jennings for fifteen years. Mickey Raphael had been Willie Nelson's harmonica player.

Moving in the Right Direction

As a teenager, Chris was an excellent student at Johnson Central High School in Paintsville, Kentucky. He graduated as the valedictorian of his class in 1996. He went on to attend Vanderbilt University in Nashville, studying engineering while he was there. However, it was his father's love of music that called to him more than his dad's profession. Chris has said that he just didn't have the desire to work in the coal mines. Instead, he decided to pursue a career as a songwriter.

It was around this time that Chris discovered bluegrass music. He and his four roommates would sit

3A 209
BIRTH OF BLUEGRASS

In December 1945, Grand Ole Opry star Bill Monroe and his mandolin brought to the Ryman Auditorium stage a band that created a new American musical form. With the banjo style of Earl Scruggs and the guitar of Lester Flatt, the new musical genre became known as "Bluegrass." Augmented by the fiddle of Chubby Wise and the bass of Howard Watts (also known as Cedric Rainwater), this ensemble became known as "The Original Bluegrass Band," which became the prototype for groups that followed.

TENNESSEE HISTORICAL COMMISSION

around at night listening to what Chris called a modern version of the genre. His favorite performers included John Hartford, Tim O'Brien, and Tony Rice. Chris and his friends also started creating some bluegrass songs themselves.

After going back and forth between Kentucky and Tennessee for a few months, Chris ultimately decided to move to Nashville for good in 2001. Knowing how talented Chris was, his uncle gave him two months' worth of living expenses to help fund the endeavor. The move was simple. Chris has said that all he took was a chair, a sleeping bag, some clothes, his guitar, and a recorder. He didn't even take a cell phone. He hated the idea of anyone knowing where he was at any given moment.

His favorite performers included John Hartford, Tim O'Brien, and Tony Rice.

After his move to Nashville, it took Chris just four days to land a songwriting contract with a music publisher. At this time he was writing as many as three songs each day. He was also making many worthwhile connections in the

music industry. Perhaps the most important one was a professional songwriter named Morgane Hayes. Although Morgane worked for a different publishing house, she had a friend who worked with Chris. After meeting him one day in 2003, Morgane began making a point of visiting her friend at work. She hoped she would run into Chris. One Friday evening he finally asked her if she would like to spend some time co-writing with him. That informal songwriting session turned into the couple's first date. By 2007, they were married.

Success and Tragedy

After writing for other artists for a while, in 2008 Chris joined a bluegrass band called The SteelDrivers. The band released their first album, *The SteelDrivers*, later that year. It seemed that Chris had as much talent for playing as he did for writing. In 2009 the International Bluegrass Music Association named The SteelDrivers as its Emerging Artist of the Year. In that year and in 2010, The SteelDrivers received a total of three Grammy nominations.

At this point, Chris had also become a father. The demands of touring made it difficult for him to spend time with his young family. He knew he needed to change something, so he chose to leave the successful group.

By this time, Chris had formed a new group—a southern rock band called the Jompson Brothers.

It seemed that Chris had as much talent for playing as he had for writing.

Chris followed up his first CMA Awards with two Grammy awards in February of 2016—Best Country Solo Performance and Best Country Album. He shares the stage with his producer, Dave Cobb.

Interestingly, none of the members was named Jompson nor related to the others. In addition to Chris, the band consisted of Greg McKee on guitar, J.T. Cure on bass, and Brad McNamee on drums.

He kept writing music for other artists, a move that helped the Jompson Brothers get more exposure. They appeared with singers such as Darius Rucker, for whom

Chris wrote "Come Back Song." They also toured as an opening act for the Zac Brown Band.

In 2013, Mercury Nashville offered Chris his own record contract. He released a single called "What Are You Listening To?" in October of that year. When it didn't do well on the charts, however, the recording company decided to cancel plans for the accompanying album. As Chris was trying to figure out his next move, he received tragic news. His father passed away due to complications from a disease called type 2 diabetes.

Chris was devastated. Wanting to help her grieving husband in any way she could, Morgane decided to take him on a road trip. She went online and bought a 1979 Jeep Cherokee, which they drove all the way from Phoenix, Arizona to Nashville, Tennessee. Morgane has said that she knew the car was a clunker, but she thought the trip would be good for them. It turned out she was right. The trip inspired Chris to write several new songs, which became the basis for his first solo album. Chris told *Billboard* magazine, "I thought a lot about music and my dad,

> Chris acquired many new fans during its rise to the top of the charts.

and the things he would have liked that I should be doing. Out of that, I actually wrote the song 'Traveller' driving down Interstate 40 through New Mexico." The song's name would also become the title of the album, which Chris recorded with the help of producer Dave Cobb.

Chris had been a fan of Cobb's for a while. He admired his work on records by Sturgill Simpson. Chris still wanted to make music that sounded like the songs he had listened to during his childhood. He hoped Cobb could help him accomplish this goal. They recorded six songs for the album after working together for only two days. The album was complete by the end of the week.

His Recent Fame

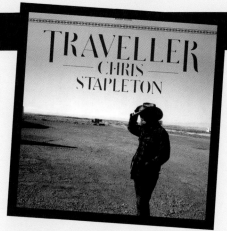

Traveller became the best-selling country album of 2016. Chris acquired many new fans during its rise to the top of the charts. His fans, along with many critics, readily praise his music. It offers something different than most contemporary country songs. One person who has yet to chime in on *Traveller*, though, is Chris's mother. He has described her as a woman of few words. She supports her son's career with great pride. When Chris performed a live concert on the *Today Show*

in July of 2017, she was cheering him on in the crowd. But Chris knows that talking about the songs he wrote following his father's death might be difficult for her. They were married for 43 years and she was still coping with the loss.

Chris doesn't let all of the rave reviews go to his head. Although he appreciates it when critics or fellow artists say nice things about his work, he knows the best thing he can do is be himself. He also knows that fame can be temporary. He has said that when people stop coming to listen to him play, he will simply keep writing songs for other artists. He still enjoys the freedom that songwriting offers him.

Chris drew a huge crowd when he performed a morning concert for NBC's *Today Show* at Rockefeller Plaza in New York City.

That Unique Style

It's not just Chris Stapleton's sound that sets him apart from other musicians today. Even the way he looks at music is different from most contemporary artists. As an experienced songwriter, Chris knows that many singers have little interest in recording a song that another artist has already recorded. Chris doesn't look at the situation that way at all. He sees his job as a performer as making a song his own through the performance. He doesn't care if that song has already been made popular by someone else. He thinks there is something special about taking a popular song and doing it a new way.

He also doesn't buy into the idea that his style is necessarily better than other ones in the world of country music. He thinks that the genre is better with variety. Chris has said that he doesn't want to put down other artists or their music. He simply wants to record his own

Chris knows that many singers have little interest in recording a song that another artist has already recorded.

and play it for people who enjoy it.

In general, Chris has become quite comfortable doing things his own way. For example, he no longer feels the need to choose between touring and his family. He and Morgane now have two children, and they accompany him when he goes on the road. Morgane's mother joins them, homeschooling the kids along the way.

It isn't unusual to see Morgane perform with her famous husband. Although she has recorded some of her own music, she has yet to release an album of her own. Occasionally, she does enjoy joining Chris on stage. She has also continued her own work as a songwriter. Her biggest success was penning "Don't Forget to Remember Me" for Carrie Underwood. Like Chris, Morgane enjoys the music but not the spotlight. In 2017, she told the *New York Times* that she thinks that is why Chris likes to grow his hair and beard so long. It offers him a small amount of privacy from everyone's eyes.

It isn't unusual to see Morgane perform with her famous husband.

Chris and Morgane perform during the 52nd Academy of Country Music Awards at T-Mobile Arena in Las Vegas, Nevada.

In an interview with *Rolling Stone*, Morgane noted how the CMA awards are just heavy pieces of glass—but glass that changes everything. Following his performance at the award show, Chris went from playing crowds of about 1,000 people to selling out concerts for thousands of fans. Sometimes the demand to see him is so high that he has to add a night to a particular venue.

Helping Others

Chris Stapleton's overwhelming success has enabled him to do some great things for others. In 2016, he headed back to Johnson Central High School on a special mission. Many of the students at Johnson Central cannot afford to buy their own instruments, so they borrow the school's band equipment. When Chris learned that many of these instruments were broken or damaged, he joined with the ACM Lifting Lives Program and the Mr. Holland's Opus Foundation to donate $57,000 worth of new instruments to the school's music program.

Band director Martina Lutz was especially touched by the gesture. She told *People* magazine that she often

Chris performs for the Country Rising Benefit Concert at Bridgestone Arena on November 12, 2017 in Nashville, Tennessee. Proceeds from the show went to support victims of the Las Vegas shooting and people in Texas, Florida, Puerto Rico and additional Caribbean islands who were impacted by the recent hurricanes.

reminds her students that Chris went to their school. To her he is proof that the students there today can go on accomplish big things in life.

While Chris was at his alma mater, he put on two free concerts. One was just for the students and teachers at Johnson Central. The second concert was for the Paintsville community. His performances helped break in the Golden Eagle Stage, a new outdoor theater at the school made possible by Ram Trucks and the company's Ram Nation volunteers.

> Chris has also used his fame to bring attention to an important cause: mental health.

Chris has also used his fame to bring attention to an important cause: mental health. The music video he recorded for his song "Fire Away" tells the story of a young woman battling severe depression. Chris hopes the video will raise awareness about mental health issues. The project was a joint venture with the Campaign to Change Direction, an organization that aims to help people recognize the symptoms of depression.

Chris released his second solo album, *From A Room*, in two volumes in 2017. He has said that while he didn't feel any pressure over the follow-up record, he did feel a big responsibility. He wanted to make sure that it lived up to the same standard as *Traveller*.

One of the things that Chris enjoyed most about playing smaller clubs at the beginning of his career was the connection he felt to the people. He doesn't want the larger size of his new venues to ruin that. He has said that one of his current goals is figuring out how to make fans seeing him perform at a stadium feel like they are actually in the front row of a club.

Chris sometimes worries that he is a one-trick pony—a term used to describe a person with only one area of expertise. He knows that artists who remain popular over time often work at re-inventing themselves to keep their

Chris sometimes worries that he is a one-trick pony—a term used to describe a person with only one area of expertise.

fans' interest. But that approach just isn't him. For now, he simply hopes that his tricks are good enough to keep the fans coming to see him play.

guitar pedal

People who meet Chris describe him as grounded and gracious. Despite all his success, he is still the same guy he was before all the attention. Although his free time is rare these days, he spends it doing things like searching online for old guitar pedals that he hopes will help him create the old sounds he loves so much. When he and Morgane get an evening together, he likes

Chris performs with Derek Mixon and Morgane at the 2017 iHeartRadio Music Festival in Las Vegas, Nevada.

to spend it visiting record stores, looking through the sales bins. Morgane doesn't seem to mind these pastimes at all. In fact, she helps by organizing his massive music library.

Everything Old is New Again

Although the songs on *From A Room: Volume 1* and *From A Room: Volume 2* are new to many fans, none of the music was written recently. Chris's "new" songs are at least two years old—some date back as many as a dozen years.

For instance, he co-wrote "Second to Know" with Mike Henderson, one of his bandmates from his SteelDrivers days.

An album can only contain so many tracks, and Chris has a long list of songs to draw from when making one. Deciding which songs to include can be challenging. This is part of why he decided to release *From A Room* in two volumes. Chris named both volumes after Nashville's Studio A, the room in which the albums were recorded.

Chris acquired many new fans during its rise to the top of the charts.

The site was once owned by RCA Records and used by such country greats as Willie Nelson, Dolly Parton, and Tammy Wynette.

Chris continues to use the same musicians as he did on his first solo album. In addition to producing the record, Dave Cobb plays acoustic guitar. Morgane also sings harmony vocals. Chris has said they took a relaxed approach when they recorded the songs on the album. They simply played what they felt like playing in the moment. This is a man who sticks with the things he likes. So far it seems to be working for him.

One of those things he likes is covering old country songs. The song, "Last Thing I Needed First Thing This Morning," is included on *From A Room*. The 1982 Willie Nelson song was a favorite of Chris's since he was a kid. He has said that he hopes he isn't the last person to record the gem. He sees it as a perfect example of how a country song should be written.

It's hard to say what will come next for Chris Stapleton. One thing is certain: it will be exactly what feels right to him. The singer isn't afraid of hard work, and he is determined to make music he is proud of. Thanks to him, an entirely new generation has been introduced to the classic sounds of old country— done the way that only Chris Stapleton can do it.

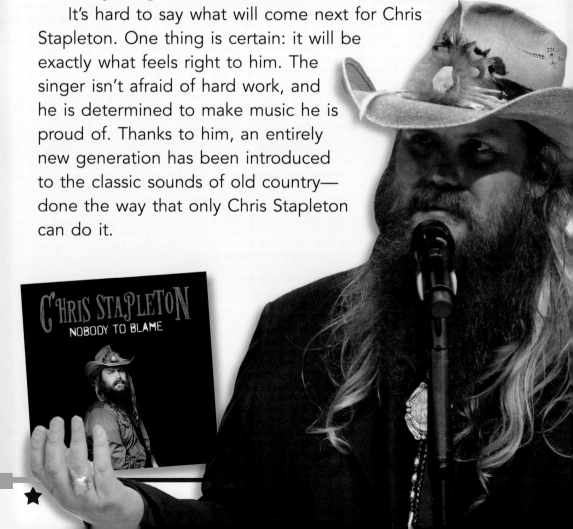

1978 Christopher Alvin Stapleton is born on April 15.

1996 Chris graduates from Johnson Central High School as the valedictorian.

2001 He moves to Nashville, landing a songwriting contract in just four days.

2007 Chris marries fellow songwriter Morgane Hayes. Chris and three other musicians form the Jompson Brothers

2008 Chris joins The SteelDrivers as lead singer.

2010 He leaves The SteelDrivers.

2013 Mercury Nashville offers Chris his own recording contract. His father passes away.

2015 Chris wins his first CMA award.

2016 Chris wins his first Grammy award as a solo artist. *Traveller* becomes the best-selling country album of the year.

2018 Chris receives Grammy nominations for Best Country Solo Performance ("Either Way"), Best Country Song ("Broken Halos," with Mike Henderson) and Best Country Album (*From A Room: Volume 1*).

2008	*The SteelDrivers*	**2017**	*From A Room:*
2010	*The Jompson Brothers*		*Volume 1*
2015	*Traveller*		*From A Room:*
			Volume 2

FURTHER READING

On the Internet

Chris Stapleton Website
   http://www.chrisstapleton.com/
Country Music Television, Chris Stapleton
   http://www.cmt.com/artists/chris-stapleton
The SteelDrivers Website
   http://www.thesteeldrivers.com/

Works Consulted

_____. "Chris Stapleton: A blazing star." CBS News, April 3, 2016.
   http://www.cbsnews.com/news/chris-stapleton-a-blazing-star/
_____. "Chris Stapleton Follows the Muse on *From a Room: Volume 1.*"
   CMT. http://www.cmt.com/news/1780950/chris-stapleton-
   follows-the-muse-on-from-a-room-volume-1/
_____. "New Music: Chris Stapleton Debut." Country Countdown
   USA, May 4, 2015. http://www.countrycountdownusa.
   com/2015/05/04/new-music-chris-stapleton-debut/
_____. "See Chris Stapleton's Whirlwind Trip Back to High School.
   Rolling Stone, April 1, 2016. http://www.rollingstone.com/music/
   news/see-chris-stapletons-whirlwind-trip-back-to-high-
   school-20160401
_____. "Why Successful People Take 10 Years to 'Succeed Overnight.'"
   Inc., May 11, 2016. https://www.inc.com/empact/why-successful-
   people-take-10-years-to-succeed-overnight.html
Anderson, Danielle. "Chris Stapleton Becomes a Hero to His High
   School — and Leaves Students in Tears." *People*, April 1, 2016.
   http://people.com/country/chris-stapleton-goes-back-to-high-
   school-and-donates-instruments/
Burchard, Jeremy. "Chris Stapleton's Former Rock Band Will Blow You
   Away." Wide Open Country, 2016. http://www.wideopencountry.
   com/chris-stapletons-former-rock-band-will-blow-away/

Caramanica, Jon. "For Chris Stapleton, A Fellow Traveller: His Wife, Morgane." *The New York Times*, May 1, 2017. https://www.nytimes.com/2017/05/01/arts/music/chris-stapleton-morgane-find-a-room-interview.html

Carter, Maria. "The Sweet Love Story Behind Country's Hottest Couple, Chris and Morgane Stapleton." *Country Living*, May 2, 2016. http://www.countryliving.com/life/entertainment/a38391/chris-and-morgane-stapleton-love-story/

Dawn Randee. "'Halo,' Chris Stapleton! Soulful country rocker heats up the Today plaza." Today, July 18, 2017. https://www.today.com/popculture/halo-chris-stapleton-soulful-country-rocker-heats-today-plaza-t113971

Dauphin, Chuck. "Chris Stapleton's Debut Album 'Traveller' Inspired by 'Soul-Searching' Road Trip." *Billboard*, April 30, 2015. http://www.billboard.com/articles/columns/the-615/6553503/chris-stapleton-debut-album-traveller-interview

Erlewine, Stephen Thomas. "Chris Stapleton." AllMusic.com. http://www.allmusic.com/artist/chris-stapleton-mn0001766237/biography

Hudak, Joseph. "Chris Stapleton: Country's Breakout Star Talks Big Year, New Music." *Rolling Stone*, December 18, 2015. http://www.rollingstone.com/music/news/chris-stapleton-countrys-breakout-star-talks-big-year-new-music-20151218

Knopper, Steve. "Chris Stapleton's success involves keeping it simple." *Chicago Tribune*, May 26, 2016. http://www.chicagotribune.com/entertainment/music/ct-chris-stapleton-ott-0527-20160524-story.html

Leahey, Andrew. "Chris Stapleton Is The Toast of the 2015 CMA Awards." *Rolling Stone*, November 4, 2015. http://www.rollingstone.com/music/news/chris-stapleton-is-the-toast-of-the-2015-cma-awards-20151104

Powers, Ann. "World Café Nashville: Chris and Morgane Stapleton."
   NPR, May 5, 2017. http://www.npr.org/sections/world-
   cafe/2017/05/05/526871785/world-cafe-nashville-chris-and-
   morgane-stapleton

Sams, Travis. "Chris Stapleton's Video for 'Fire Away' Not What You
   Would Expect." WKDQ, March 1, 2016. http://wkdq.com/chris-
   stapletons-video-for-fire-away-not-what-you-would-expect/

Shelburne, Craig. "The Unsung Heroism of Chris Stapleton." *American
   Songwriter*, July 21, 2014. https://americansongwriter.
   com/2014/07/5-nashvilles-finest-chris-stapleton-songwriter/

Tannenbaum, Rob. "Chris Stapleton on Being the Accidental Country
   Star: 'The Lesson is, Make the Music that You Love.'" *Billboard*,
   February 4, 2016. http://www.billboard.com/articles/news/
   magazine-feature/6866048/chris-stapleton-grammys-on-traveller-
   success

Thompson, Gayle. "Chris Stapleton Says His Father Influenced
   'Traveller' Album." The Boot, February 9, 2016.
   http://theboot.com/chris-stapleton-father-influenced-traveller/

Vain, Madison. "Chris Stapleton breaks down his latest opus, *From a
   Room*." *Entertainment Weekly*, May 5, 2017. http://ew.com/
   music/2017/05/05/chris-stapleton-from-a-room-interview/

Welch, Will. "The GQ&A: Chris Stapleton, Country Music's Cinderella
   Story and Grammy's Dark Horse." *GQ*, January 7, 2016.
   https://www.gq.com/story/chris-stapleton-grammy-interview

Whitaker, Sterling. "Chris Stapleton's Father Passes Away." The Boot,
   October 7, 2013. http://theboot.com/chris-stapleton-father-dies/

Yahr, Emily. "A year after Chris Stapleton's CMAs shocker, country
   music is still wondering how much it mattered." *The Washington
   Post*, October 31, 2016. https://www.washingtonpost.com/
   lifestyle/style/a-year-after-chris-stapletons-cmas-shocker-country-
   music-is-still-wondering-how-much-it-mattered/2016/10/28/
   fb4c8648-9c5a-11e6-b3c9-f662adaa0048_story.html

★ INDEX ★